Explore the Universe

QUASARS AND BLACK HOLES

WORLD BOOK

a Scott Fetzer company
Chicago
www.worldbookonline.com

World Book, Inc.
233 N. Michigan Avenue
Chicago, IL 60601
U.S.A.

For information about other World Book publications, visit our
Web site at **http://www.worldbookonline.com** or call
1-800-WORLDBK (967-5325).

For information about sales to schools and
libraries, call **1-800-975-3250 (United States),**
or **1-800-837-5365 (Canada).**

Library of Congress Cataloging-in-Publication data
Quasars and black holes.
    p. cm. -- (Explore the universe)
    Summary: "An introduction to quasars and black holes with
information about their formation and characteristics. Includes
diagrams, fun facts, a glossary, a resource list, and an index"
-- Provided by publisher.
    Includes index.
    ISBN 978-0-7166-9552-3
    1. Black holes (Astronomy)--Juvenile literature. 2. Quasars--
Juvenile literature. I. World Book, Inc.
    QB843.B55.Q37 2010
    523.8'875--dc22
                        2009040183

ISBN 978-0-7166-9544-8 (set)
Printed in China by Leo Paper Products LTD.,
  Heshan, Guangdong
1st printing February 2010

STAFF
Executive Committee:
President: Paul A. Gazzolo
Vice President and Chief Marketing Officer:
  Patricia Ginnis
Vice President and Chief Financial Officer:
  Donald D. Keller
Vice President and Editor in Chief: Paul A. Kobasa
Vice President, Licensing & Business Development:
  Richard Flower
Managing Director, International: Benjamin Hinton
Director, Human Resources: Bev Ecker
Chief Technology Officer: Tim Hardy

Editorial:
Associate Director, Supplementary Publications:
  Scott Thomas
Managing Editor, Supplementary Publications:
  Barbara A. Mayes
Senior Editor, Supplementary Publications:
  Kristina A. Vaicikonis
Manager, Research, Supplementary Publications:
  Cheryl Graham
Manager, Contracts & Compliance
  (Rights & Permissions): Loranne K. Shields
Editors: Michael DuRoss, Brian Johnson
Writer: Rebecca Hankin
Indexer: David Pofelski

Graphics and Design:
Manager: Tom Evans
Coordinator, Design Development
  and Production: Brenda B. Tropinski
Senior Designer: Isaiah Sheppard
Photographs Editor: Kathy Creech

Pre-Press and Manufacturing:
Director: Carma Fazio
Manufacturing Manager: Steven K. Hueppchen
Production/Technology Manager: Anne Fritzinger
Proofreader: Emilie Schrage

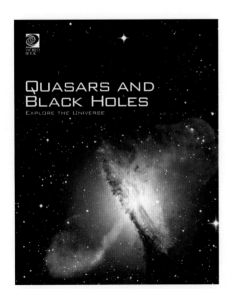

Cover image:
A jet of high-energy particles
traveling at about half the
speed of light blasts from a
black hole in the galaxy
Centaurus A. The jet extends
some 13,000 light-years
into space.

NASA/CXC/CfA/R.Kraft et al. (x-ray),
MPIfR/ESO/APEX/A.Weiss et al.
(submillimeter), ESO/WFI (optical)

CONTENTS

If a word is printed in **bold letters that look like this,** that word's meaning is given in the glossary on pages 60-61.

INTRODUCTION

Black holes are infinitely dense, infinitely dark, and infinitely fascinating. Astronomer John Wheeler, who popularized the term "black hole," said, "[The black hole] teaches us that space can be crumpled like a piece of paper into an infinitesimal dot, that time can be extinguished like a blown-out flame, and that the laws of physics that we regard as 'sacred' ... are anything but." Forever hidden from human eyes, black holes are still a constant source of study and speculation. The extreme gravity produced by a black hole challenges not only our understanding of basic physics but also the larger universe in general.

Eta Carinae, a star that is from 100 to 150 times as massive as the sun, will probably end its life as a black hole. The doomed star is giving off huge amounts of dust and gas (colorized in purple) in what astronomers believe are the last stages before exploding in a brilliant supernova. The star's core will then collapse under the weight of its own gravitational force.

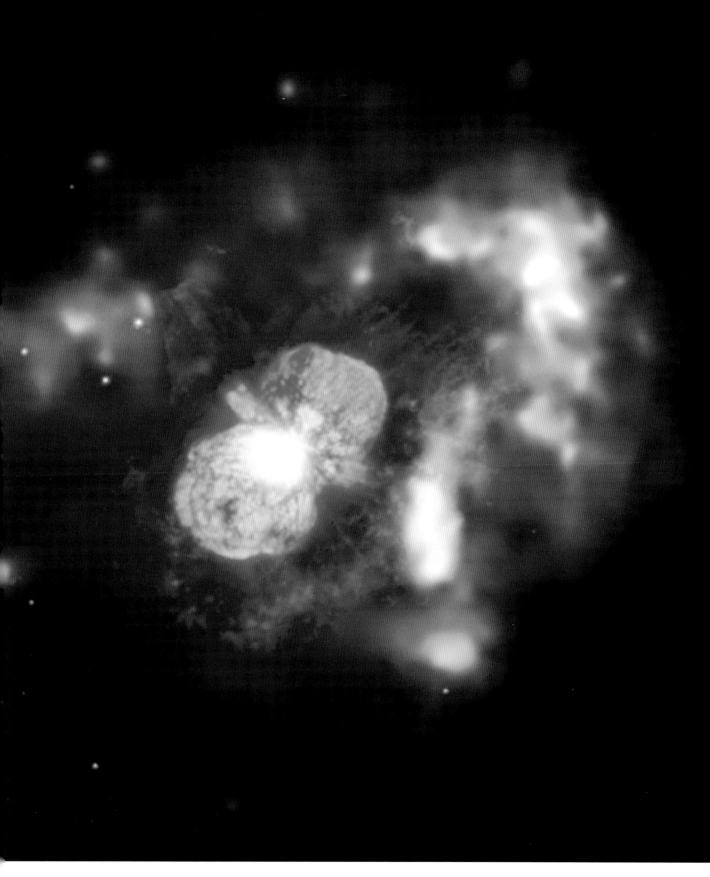

WHAT ARE BLACK HOLES?

THE ULTIMATE TRAP

One of the strangest objects in the universe is a **black hole.** Scientists think a black hole forms when a supergiant **star** collapses from the force of its own **gravity.** It leaves behind an extremely dense **core** that is more than three times the **mass** of the sun. This core collapses even further, forming an invisible center with an extremely strong gravitational pull. Anything that gets within a certain distance of a black hole, even light, is captured forever.

As a black hole pulls matter toward itself, the matter is drawn into a large spinning whirlpool. The matter continues to spin closer and closer to the black hole's center, eventually being sucked into it.

Beginning in the late 1700's, mathematical calculations had pointed to the possible existence of tiny, gravity-dense objects that could trap light. By the 1900's, findings about the nature of gravity had led many scientists to accept that such objects should exist. But it wasn't until 1967 that the American physicist John Archibald Wheeler popularized the name *black hole.*

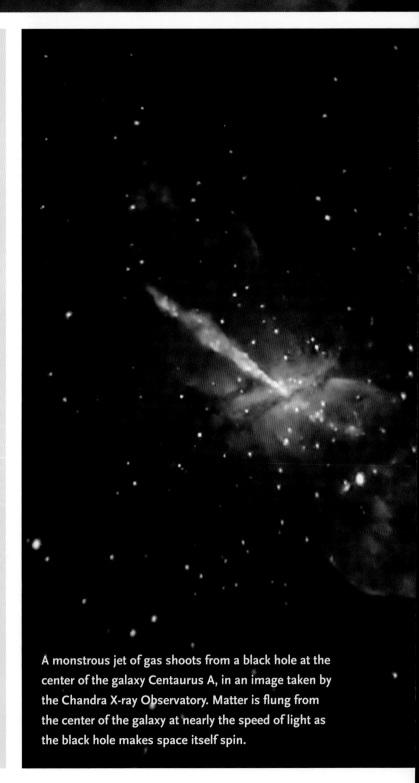

A monstrous jet of gas shoots from a black hole at the center of the galaxy Centaurus A, in an image taken by the Chandra X-ray Observatory. Matter is flung from the center of the galaxy at nearly the speed of light as the black hole makes space itself spin.

A black hole is an area of space where gravity is so strong that anything that gets too close, even light, becomes trapped and can never escape from it.

The American physicist John Archibald Wheeler was the first person to popularize the term *black hole*.

The black hole at the center of the Milky Way Galaxy is an estimated 27 million miles (44 million kilometers) in diameter.

Huge stars, each as big as the sun, are being pulled apart as they whip around a black hole at speeds up to 20,000 miles (32,000 kilometers) per second, in an artist's illustration. The black hole is about as large as the orbit of Mercury.

HOW A BLACK HOLE FORMS

A black hole is created after a massive star explodes. According to the theory of general relativity developed by physicist Albert Einstein, a black hole can form when a massive star runs out of nuclear fuel and is crushed by its own gravitational force. As long as a star burns fuel, it creates an outward push that balances the inward pull of gravity. When all the fuel has been used up, the star can no longer support its own weight. As a result, the core of the star collapses. If the *mass* (amount of matter) of the core is at least three times that of the sun, the core collapses into a space smaller than an atom in a fraction of a second.

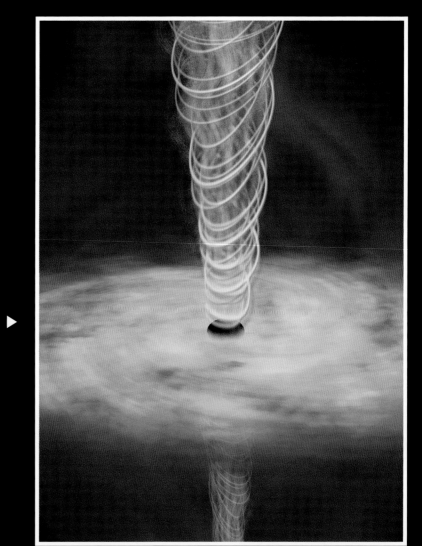

Beams of matter and energy ▶ shoot from a black hole in the center of a galaxy in an artist's illustration. The temperature of the surrounding disk of gas and dust grows hotter as it nears the black hole, represented by the change in color.

Massive lobes of gas and dust erupt ▶
from the star Eta Carinae in an image
taken by the Hubble Space Telescope.
The core of Eta Carinae, like those of
other supermassive stars, will likely be
crushed by its own gravitational force
and become a black hole.

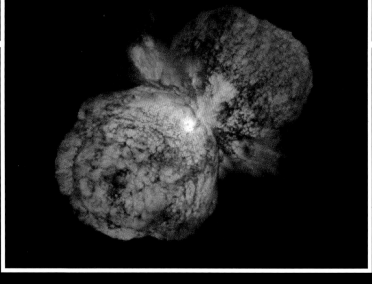

▼ Although most of the nearby gas is
sucked into the black hole, some gas
escapes in jets that erupt out into space at
nearly the speed of light.

▼ Over time, the jets hollow out huge
cavities in the gaseous atmosphere
surrounding the black hole.

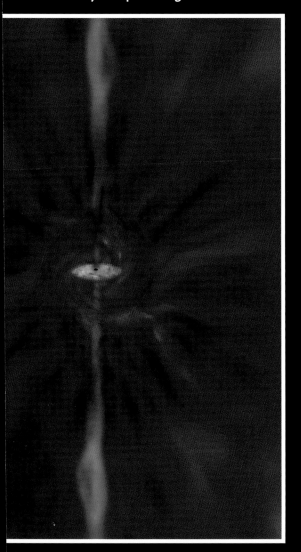

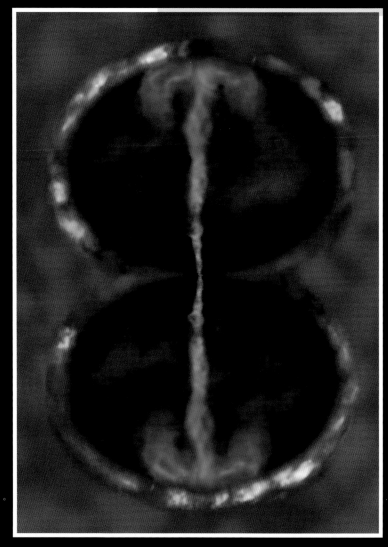

HOW DO WE KNOW BLACK HOLES EXIST?

THE EVIDENCE MOUNTS

We cannot see **black holes** because nothing, not even light, can escape them. They truly are black—and invisible. No one has ever discovered a black hole for certain. To prove that a compact object is a black hole, scientists would have to measure effects that only a black hole could produce. The German-born American physicist Albert Einstein predicted that some strange effects would occur due to the strong gravitational field of a black hole. One such effect would be a severe bending of a light beam. Another would be an extreme slowing of time. But astronomers have found compact objects that are almost certainly black holes.

As gas and other matter are pulled into the orbit of a black hole, it gives off **X rays** and **radio waves.** Powerful **observatories** can pick up these signals and so identify the location of the black holes. Another method of looking for them is by observing the movement of **stars** around a suspected black hole. If the stars are being pulled by an invisible but strong gravitational field, they may be close to a black hole. Scientists have found evidence that there are probably billions of black holes in the universe.

Physicist Albert Einstein, who predicted the existence of black holes in his theories of relativity, discusses research with astronomer Charles St. John at the Mount Wilson Observatory in California in 1931. Much of St. John's work focused on confirming Einstein's general theory of relativity.

"NO POWER, NO SCIENCE"

Scientists at the control center for the Chandra X-ray Observatory monitor the data the telescope collects and tell the telescope what to observe.

Scientists can determine the presence of a black hole because of the matter being pulled in by the black hole's gravity.

Cygnus X-1

Radio jet

The brilliance of Cygnus X-1, regarded as the first black hole ever discovered, is revealed in a composite image taken by the Isaac Newton Telescope in the Canary Islands. A jet of matter and radio energy given off by the powerful black hole appears in the inset.

TELESCOPIC EVIDENCE OF BLACK HOLES

Black holes really are black. Because no light can escape a black hole, astronomers cannot see one directly. One way to "see" a black hole is by looking at its effect on objects nearby.

In their search for black holes, astronomers also may focus on a particular area of space giving off high levels of energy. Scientists believe that some sources of high-energy electromagnetic waves are the clouds of gas surrounding a black hole. They believe that just before gas and dust reach the point of no return—called the event horizon—this cloud of particles gets so hot it glows. Scientists suspect that a black hole may be at the center of this ball of glowing dust and gas.

The incredible gravity of a black hole traps any object that gets too close. This intense gravity can provide clues about whether a dark patch of space is empty or is really a black hole. By watching the motion of stars and debris orbiting near a suspected black hole, physicists can determine if a strong gravitational field is affecting the way they move. If these objects seem to be orbiting around "nothing," they may be orbiting a black hole.

IMAGES OF THE GALAXY CENTAURUS A BY VARIOUS TELESCOPES

Different wavelengths of light can reveal features not visible to the unaided eye. The type of light being gathered can provide information about the kinds of chemicals in a certain area or feature, as well as its temperature. For example, an X-ray image of the galaxy Centaurus A (right, above) shows a ring of gas heated to several million degrees surrounding the black hole at the center. Jets of radio waves being ejected from the black hole are apparent in images made by a radio telescope (right and far right).

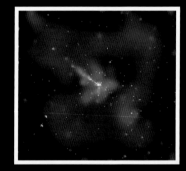

Chandra X ray

DSS Optical

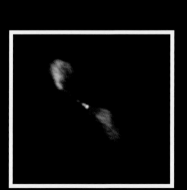

NRAO RADIO CONTINUUM

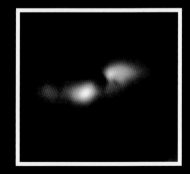

NRAO RADIO (21-CM)

▲ A composite image of Centaurus A based on information from several telescopes reveals many aspects of the galaxy's black hole at once, including chemical makeup and temperature.

WHAT IS A SINGULARITY?

THE CENTER OF GRAVITY

The force of **gravity** at a **black hole's singularity** is so strong that all matter entering it collapses. According to the chief theory about black holes, the matter then becomes concentrated in a single point. A singularity takes up less space than a single atom. In fact, some mathematical calculations suggest that a singularity has no volume at all. Yet it has incredible **mass.** The result is that the singularity has infinite density. This concept can be difficult to understand. Singularities also puzzle scientists, because the known laws of physics don't seem to apply. For example, scientists do not yet understand how the density of such a small point could be so great.

According to the general theory of relativity developed by the German-born American scientist Albert Einstein, time and space are not absolutely separate. The theory refers to them instead as a single entity, called space-time. This entity is a combination of the dimension of time and the three dimensions of space—length, width, and height. Thus, space-time is four-dimensional. The gravity of a black hole is so great that it can warp space-time. If an outside observer were able to look inside a black hole's **event horizon** they would see time slow down.

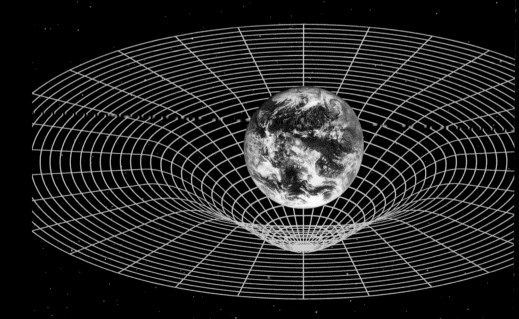

The Earth *distorts* (bends) space-time around it. This curve in the fabric of space causes objects near Earth to be pulled toward us. The closer an object comes, the greater is the distortion in space-time and the faster the object is pulled toward Earth.

A singularity is the center of a black hole. Everything that gets pulled into a black hole ends up in the singularity.

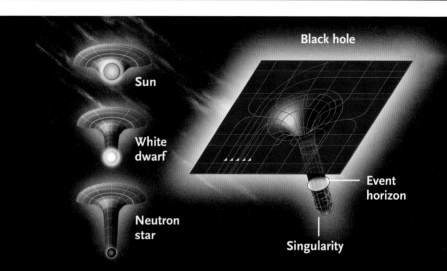

The greater the *mass* (amount of matter) of an object, the greater its effect on the space around it. That is, objects with greater mass create deeper "holes" in space-time. For this reason, a black hole distorts space-time more than the sun.

Sun

White dwarf

Neutron star

Black hole

Event horizon

Singularity

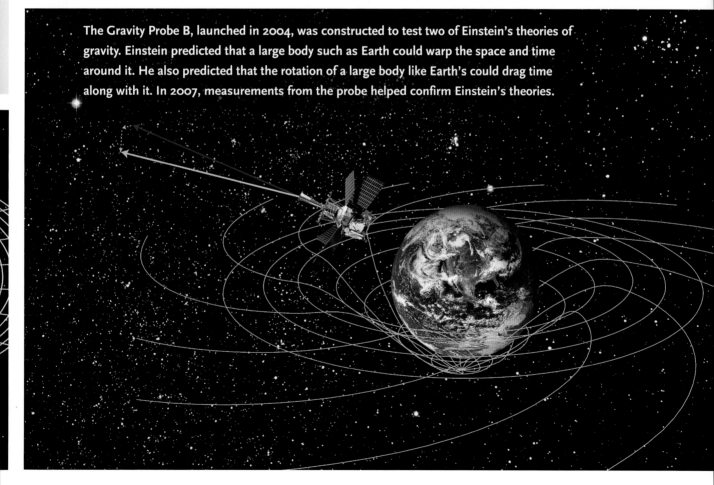

The Gravity Probe B, launched in 2004, was constructed to test two of Einstein's theories of gravity. Einstein predicted that a large body such as Earth could warp the space and time around it. He also predicted that the rotation of a large body like Earth's could drag time along with it. In 2007, measurements from the probe helped confirm Einstein's theories.

WHAT IS AN EVENT HORIZON?

THE POINT OF NO RETURN

The **event horizon** is the surface of a **black hole.** However, it is not the type of surface you can see or touch. At the event horizon, the force of **gravity** becomes strong enough to overcome any other force. Light and matter that cross the event horizon become trapped by the black hole's tremendous gravitational pull. Matter can exist at the event horizon for only a mere instant until it rushes into the **singularity** at the speed of light. An event horizon, therefore, might be thought of as the edge or boundary of a black hole.

The more *mass* (amount of matter) the black hole has, the farther the event horizon is from its singularity. In the case of supermassive black holes, an event horizon may extend for billions of miles.

DID YOU KNOW?

The idea of an object so dense that not even light could escape was proposed as far back as the early 1800's.

IF EARTH WERE A BLACK HOLE

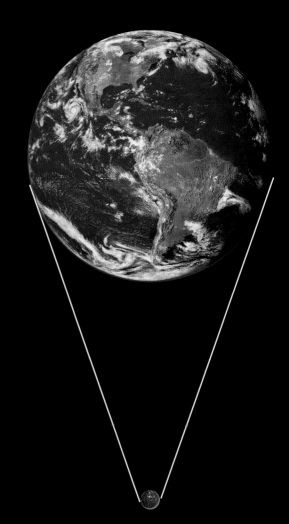

If a star with the same mass as Earth collapsed and became a black hole, its event horizon would be only as large as a marble.

An event horizon is a gravitational boundary surrounding a black hole. Anything moving closer to a black hole than the event horizon cannot escape.

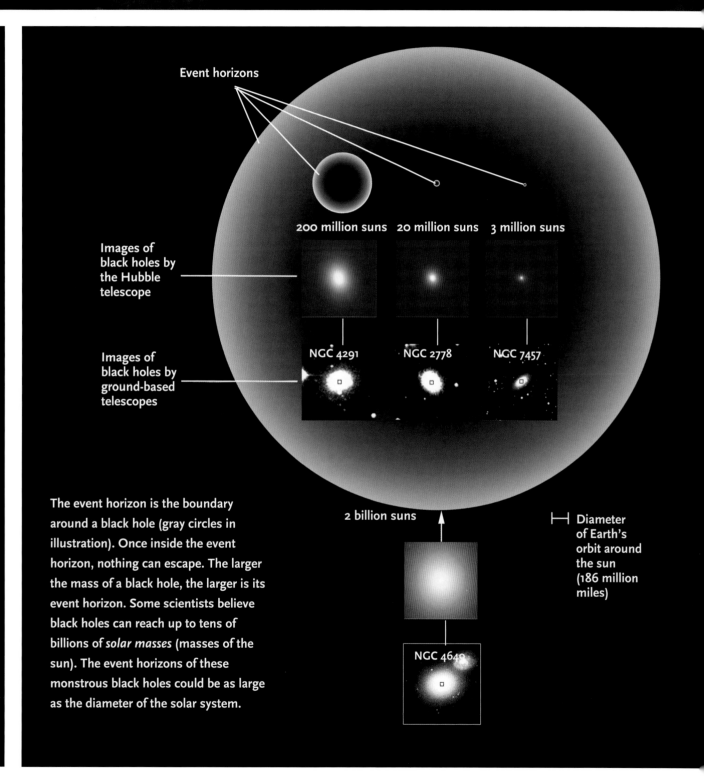

Event horizons

200 million suns   20 million suns   3 million suns

Images of black holes by the Hubble telescope

NGC 4291   NGC 2778   NGC 7457

Images of black holes by ground-based telescopes

2 billion suns

The event horizon is the boundary around a black hole (gray circles in illustration). Once inside the event horizon, nothing can escape. The larger the mass of a black hole, the larger is its event horizon. Some scientists believe black holes can reach up to tens of billions of *solar masses* (masses of the sun). The event horizons of these monstrous black holes could be as large as the diameter of the solar system.

Diameter of Earth's orbit around the sun (186 million miles)

NGC 4649

WHAT HAPPENS OUTSIDE THE EVENT HORIZON?

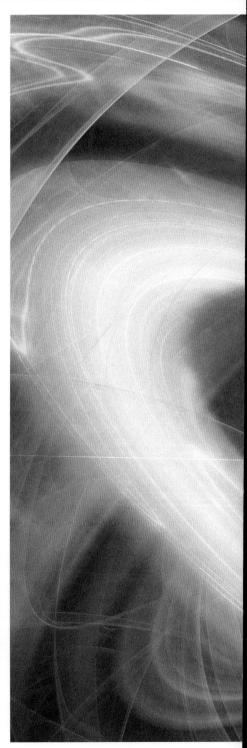

THE VISIBLE BLACK HOLE

As a **black hole's gravity** pulls matter closer and closer, a spiraling disk forms. This is called the **accretion disk.** Matter within the accretion disk orbits the black hole like water spiraling toward a sink drain. Matter in the disk is close enough to be affected by the black hole's gravity but has not reached the point of no return.

Eventually, most of the matter in the accretion disk reaches the **event horizon** and is pulled into the **singularity.**

Powerful radiation, such as **X rays** and **infrared light,** is given off around the event horizon. This radiation is one way astronomers can observe a black hole. Because no light can escape from inside the event horizon, astronomers can only study what happens on the outside of the event horizon.

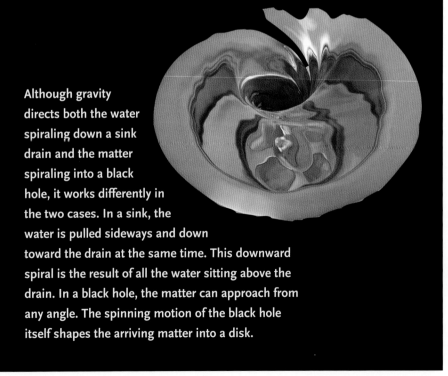

Although gravity directs both the water spiraling down a sink drain and the matter spiraling into a black hole, it works differently in the two cases. In a sink, the water is pulled sideways and down toward the drain at the same time. This downward spiral is the result of all the water sitting above the drain. In a black hole, the matter can approach from any angle. The spinning motion of the black hole itself shapes the arriving matter into a disk.

Outside the event horizon, hot gases and other matter form a spiraling disk.

Matter spiraling into a black hole produces jets of X rays that shoot outward in an artist's illustration. These X rays provide one sign astronomers use to detect a black hole.

WHAT HAPPENS TO MATTER ONCE IT ENTERS A BLACK HOLE?

THE POINT OF NO RETURN

We cannot see anything that has passed inside the **event horizon** of a **black hole,** because the black hole is truly black. Not even light can escape it. Still, scientists have developed theories about what happens to matter once it is sucked into a black hole. Scientists believe that all matter collects and is compressed inside the **singularity.** Of course, the matter would look very different from the way it appeared before entering the black hole. The intensity of the black hole's **gravity** would surely cause all objects, large and small, to undergo a tremendous change. The objects would probably be ripped into the smallest particles of matter and become part of the singularity.

DID YOU KNOW?

The supermassive black hole at the center of the Milky Way is believed to be 4 million times as massive as the sun.

GOING, GOING, GONE

The intensity of ultraviolet light *emitted* (given off) by an object falling into a black hole varies, when observed from Earth, as it moves closer to the event horizon.

An object or blob of matter circling a black hole (1) appears relatively bright in ultraviolet (UV) light. As the blob moves to the far side of the event horizon (2), most of the UV light is blocked. When the object reappears on the near side of

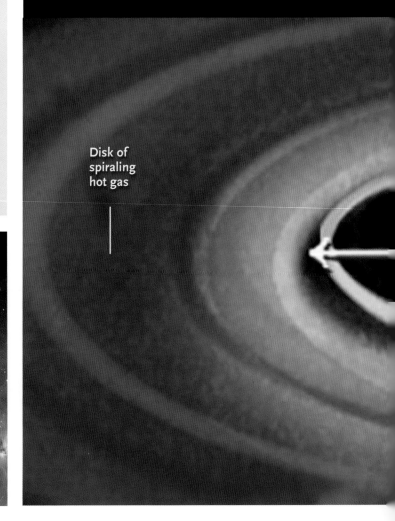

Disk of spiraling hot gas

No one knows for sure what happens to matter after it enters a black hole.

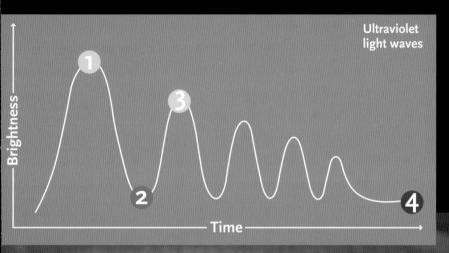

Ultraviolet light waves

Brightness

Time

the event horizon (3), the UV light becomes brighter. But because the object is closer to the black hole, the light is not as bright as it was before. After several more rotations around the event horizon (4), the object and its light disappear into the black hole.

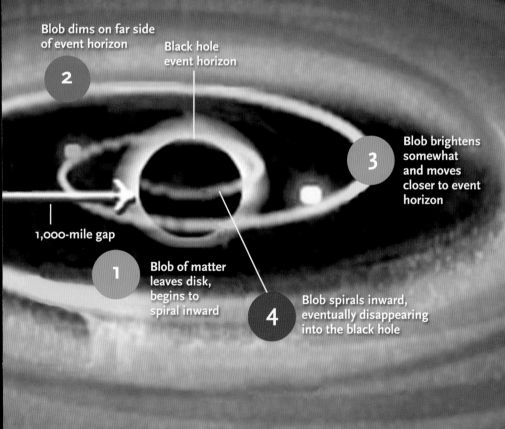

Blob dims on far side of event horizon

2

Black hole event horizon

1,000-mile gap

1 Blob of matter leaves disk, begins to spiral inward

3 Blob brightens somewhat and moves closer to event horizon

4 Blob spirals inward, eventually disappearing into the black hole

THE EVENT HORIZON TELLS A TALE

The **singularity** of a **black hole** has no volume. At the same time, it has tremendous *mass* (amount of matter). The size of a black hole's **event horizon** varies according to the mass of the singularity. The German scientist Karl Schwarzschild (1873–1916) discovered a mathematical relationship between the mass of an object and its event horizon. The radius of an event horizon was named the **Schwarzschild radius** in his honor. It is also used as the standard measure of how big a black hole is.

The Schwarzschild radii of some black holes are only about 100 miles (160 kilometers). However, the Schwarzchild radius of a supermassive black hole varies from a few million to several billion miles. To get a sense of how big this is, keep in mind that the average distance between the sun and the farthest **planet** in the **solar system,** Neptune, is less than 3 billion miles. In other words, a supermassive black hole could be wider than the orbit of Neptune.

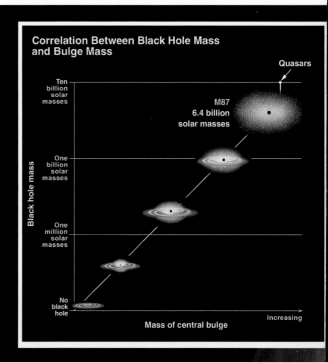

Correlation Between Black Hole Mass and Bulge Mass

Quasars

Ten billion solar masses

M87 6.4 billion solar masses

One billion solar masses

Black hole mass

One million solar masses

No black hole

Mass of central bulge — Increasing

The *mass* (amount of matter) of a black hole located in the center of a galaxy is directly related to its bulge, the material that surrounds it. The larger the bulge, the larger the black hole.

DID YOU KNOW?

Astronomers believe the massive star Eta Carinae will explode in a supernova that will appear as bright as the moon in Earth's skies.

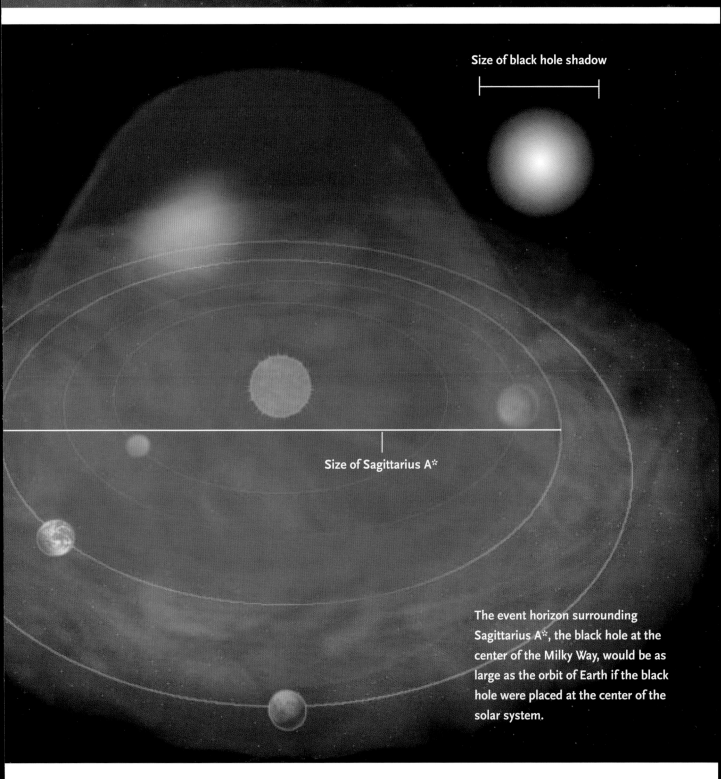

Size of black hole shadow

Size of Sagittarius A*

The event horizon surrounding
Sagittarius A*, the black hole at the
center of the Milky Way, would be as
large as the orbit of Earth if the black
hole were placed at the center of the
solar system.

FOCUS ON

POWERHOUSE GALAXIES

Since the discovery of quasars, scientists have found other galaxies that give off a tremendous amount of electromagnetic energy from their centers. Not all of these galaxies give off the same kinds of energy. Some galaxies, called radio galaxies, give off radio waves, and others give off X rays. Most of these galaxies give off several different types of energy. All galaxies of this kind are called active galaxies. Their centers are called active galactic nuclei (AGN's). Astronomers believe black holes power AGN's. Some of the matter being pulled into the black hole is shot out as jets of matter and radiation that can be seen across the universe. How black holes produce these jets is mostly a mystery to scientists.

Many astronomers believe AGN's are in galaxies that formed early in the history of the universe. These galaxies had much more dust and gas floating freely than a mature galaxy such as the

Radiation given off by a black ▶ hole heats a halo of gas and dust surrounding the center of the Circinus Galaxy, an active galaxy about 13 million light-

Milky Way. Scientists believe this extra gas and dust fell into a black hole at the center of the galaxy. The material began to heat up and give off electromagnetic energy in unparalleled amounts.

Most of the gas and dust in our galaxy has been used to form planets and stars. So the Milky Way does not have the "fuel" to power an AGN. Some scientists think the Milky Way may have been an active galaxy earlier in its history, but no one knows for sure. Scientists have observed a large mass of matter moving toward the black hole at the center of the Milky Way. Although the matter will not hit the core for millions of years, it is believed this mass will temporarily turn the Milky Way into an active galaxy.

A normal spiral galaxy similar to our own Milky Way appears as a disk with a slight bulge in the middle. The light coming from the middle appears brighter than the rest of the galaxy. The Milky Way has a relatively inactive galactic nucleus.

A galaxy with an active galactic nucleus (AGN) can have a central bulge many times brighter than the rest of the galaxy.

Some AGN's are so bright that the light from the quasar in the central bulge can drown out the light from the rest of the galaxy.

WHAT IS A SUPERMASSIVE BLACK HOLE?

THE GALACTIC CORE

Scientists think that most **galaxies** have a supermassive **black hole** at their center. These black holes probably formed by swallowing immense quantities of gas over billions of years. Using the Hubble Space Telescope, scientists have determined the speed of gas spinning around a supermassive black hole to be greater than 930,000 miles (1.5 billion kilometers) per hour.

Astronomers believe that a supermassive black hole is at the center of our galaxy. It is known as Sagittarius A* because it can be found within the constellation Sagittarius in the night sky. Having observed rapidly moving stars surrounding Sagittarius A*, scientists concluded that only a black hole's **gravity** could account for the stars' motion.

The black hole at the center of the Milky Way Galaxy is known as Sagittarius A*. This black hole has 4 million times as much mass as the sun.

Lobe of hot gas

Sgr A*

Galactic plane

Lobe of hot gas

DID YOU KNOW?

If the sun became a black hole and Earth were the same distance from the sun as it is today, the gravity of the sun/black hole would not be strong enough to pull Earth out of its orbit.

Individual spots of light captured in an image by the Chandra X-ray Observatory likely represent galaxies with supermassive black holes at their centers. These black holes may be billions of times as massive as the sun.

Quasars powered by supermassive black holes (blue circles), dating from the early history of the universe, are revealed in a 2007 image taken by the Spitzer Space Telescope. The discovery of the distant quasars, long theorized by astronomers, provided direct evidence that quasars were far more common in the early universe than they are today.

ARE THERE DIFFERENT TYPES OF BLACK HOLES?

The Andromeda Galaxy, like the Milky Way, is believed to have a supermassive black hole at its center. Andromeda, which is from 2.5 million to 3 million light-years from Earth, is the closest large galaxy to the Milky Way.

In physical appearance, black holes differ only in size.

THE SIZE MATTERS

Some **black holes** are larger than others, but all black holes seem to behave in the same way. However, scientists sometimes call a black hole by a different name based on *where* it appears. Astronomers agree that most, if not all, **galaxies** have a black hole at their center. These are called galactic *nuclei* (cores). Some galaxies are more active than others, giving off more energy from their nucleus. During periods of extreme activity, the nucleus radiates more energy than does the rest of the stars, gas, and dust in the entire galaxy.

Astronomers call these black holes **active galactic nuclei** or AGN's. Scientists usually refer to a black hole that is not at the center of a galaxy simply as a black hole.

Scientists believe that the Milky Way Galaxy contains millions of black holes. They vary in size from a few **solar masses** to scores of solar masses. A solar mass is equal to the **mass** (amount of matter) of the sun. The nearest black hole to Earth is about 1,600 **light-years** away, in the constellation Sagittarius.

A black hole is surrounded by a disk of material (blue and green) and a cloud of debris farther out called a torus (orange). Some large supermassive black holes produce jets of matter and energy from their cores (white).

Disk and torus around biggest black holes (more than 100 million suns)

Less active and smaller black holes may still have a torus (orange) but lack the energy jets of their larger cousins.

Disk and torus around smaller black holes (less than 100 million suns)

DO BLACK HOLES EVER EXIST IN PAIRS?

Black holes can be a part of a *binary* (two-star) system. In some cases, the more massive black hole "cannibalizes" its partner, as shown in an artist's illustration.

DID YOU KNOW?

Black holes are not the only objects to steal matter from their binary partner. Some small dense stars, such as white dwarfs and neutron stars, may do the same. In the case of a white dwarf, this stolen matter can eventually build up, leading to a massive supernova explosion.

Many black holes are part of a binary star system. A binary star system is really two stars that hold each other captive by the force of gravity, with each orbiting around the other.

A HUNGRY PARTNER

Black holes often occur as part of a **binary star** system. In this case, a black hole and a normal **star** orbit one another closely. Because the black hole is so powerful, its **gravity** pulls gas and other matter away from the normal star, sucking it toward its center at a faster and faster speed. Over time, the black hole's *mass* (amount of matter) increases while the mass of the normal star decreases. Most of the known black holes in our own **galaxy** are in binary star systems.

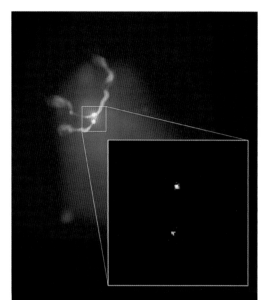

Jets of radio waves (above, colorized in pink) from two supermassive black holes (inset) pierce a cloud of superhot gas in the galaxy cluster Abell 400. The black holes are spiraling toward each other and should eventually merge.

Two black holes orbit each other in a binary system in an artist's illustration of a rare finding by the Sloan Digital Sky Survey. The black holes orbit the system's center of mass every 100 years at a speed of 3,700 miles (6,000 kilometers) per second. The smaller of the black holes has 20 times as much mass as the sun; the larger, 50 times as much.

COULD THE SUN EVER BECOME A BLACK HOLE?

A QUIET ENDING

Our sun is a medium-sized **star.** In order for it to become a **black hole,** it would have to be a giant star with 11 times as much *mass* (amount of matter). It is this tremendous mass that causes a star to collapse at the end of its life, turning into a black hole.

Instead of becoming a black hole, our sun will eventually diminish as it reaches the final stages of its existence. Low-mass stars like the sun gradually blast away their outer layers. Without fuel, nuclear fusion reactions in the **core** end, leaving behind a glowing ball called a **white dwarf.** (Fusion is the combination of two or more atomic *nuclei* [cores] to form the nucleus of a heavier element.) Nuclear fusion releases the energy that powers stars.

Scientists estimate that the sun will collapse into a white dwarf about 5 billion years from now. Eventually this core will cease to produce energy altogether. At this point it will become a **black dwarf.**

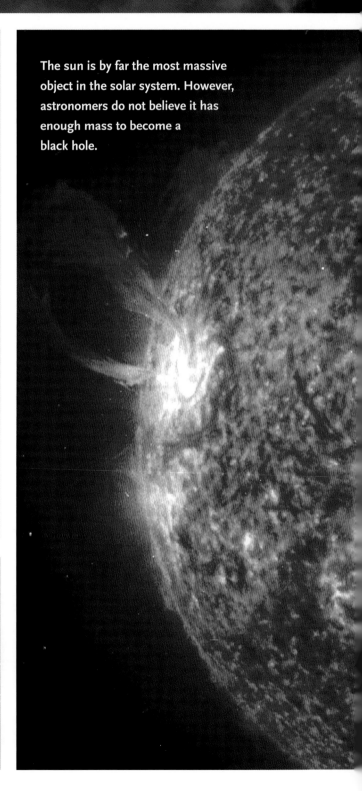

The sun is by far the most massive object in the solar system. However, astronomers do not believe it has enough mass to become a black hole.

Our own sun could never become a black hole because it doesn't have enough mass.

A ring of gas heated to 54,000 °F (30,000 °C) surrounds a dying star about 5,000 light-years from Earth. The star is contracting and becoming a white dwarf after using up its fuel.

Scientists believe a star ends its life in one of three ways. If a star has a relatively low mass, it will become a white dwarf. If it has a higher mass, it will explode in a violent supernova. Some supernova stars become neutron stars. Stars with the highest mass will become black holes.

Low- to average-mass star → → White dwarf

Large-mass star → → Neutron star

Very large-mass star → → Black hole

REDSHIFT

Much of the light that we observe from objects in space shows redshift, or a shift in the spectrum toward longer, redder wavelengths. There are two main causes of redshift. When a heavenly body is moving away from us, the Doppler effect stretches its light toward redder wavelengths. This effect is called Doppler redshift. You may have noticed the Doppler effect when a train blows its whistle. The pitch of a train whistle seems higher when the train approaches and lower after it passes. The actual pitch of the whistle remains constant, but the Doppler effect shifts its wavelength. The other cause of redshift is the expansion of the universe itself. This effect is called cosmological redshift.

When astronomers discuss redshift, they are usually referring to cosmological redshift rather than Doppler redshift. Scientists believe that since the big bang 13.7 billion years ago, the universe has expanded from a single point to its present size. As the universe expands, it stretches light traveling through space, much as a spring is stretched as its ends are pulled apart. The farther light has traveled, the more cosmological redshift it shows. Light from the most distant galaxies shows the strongest redshift. Such light has been stretched so much that it arrives as infrared or radio waves. By measuring redshift, astronomers can measure the distance to faraway galaxies.

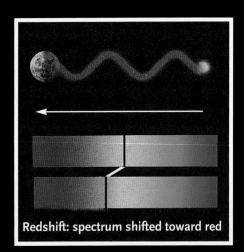

Redshift: spectrum shifted toward red

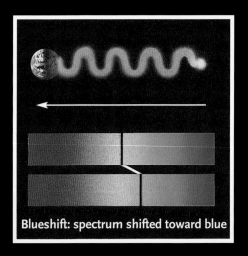

Blueshift: spectrum shifted toward blue

▲
Astronomers observe redshift more often than blueshift because most objects in the universe are moving away from Earth, not toward it.

Galaxies dating from as early as 13 billion years ago glow in a ▶ composite photograph created using images from the Hubble Space Telescope and the two Keck telescopes on Mauna Kea, Hawaii. The light from the farthest of these galaxies shows some of the greatest redshift ever observed.

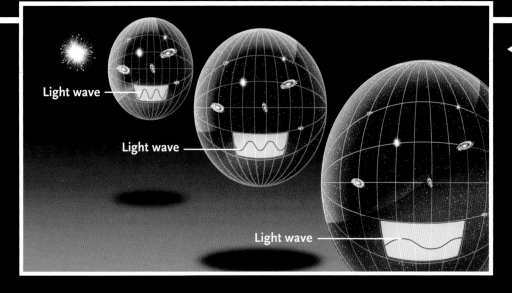

Light wave

Light wave

Light wave

◀ Objects located far outside our galaxy are moving away from us. The light from these objects is shifted toward the longer, redder end of the spectrum because of cosmological redshift. That is, as the universe expands, it stretches the light from these distant objects, increasing its wavelength.

WHAT ARE QUASARS?

THE CENTRAL STAR

The word **quasar** is short for *quasi-stellar radio source*. The term *quasi-stellar* means *star-like* and refers to the fact that quasars often resemble **stars** in the Milky Way, our own **galaxy.** In reality, quasars are far beyond our galaxy. They are some of the most distant objects we are able to observe in the universe.

Astronomers believe each quasar is powered by a giant **black hole** that produces energy by swallowing clouds of gas from the surrounding galaxy. Quasars give off more energy than any other object in the universe. Some quasars shine a trillion times more brightly than the sun. The energy from a quasar takes different forms. One form is **visible light**. Other types of quasar energy are not visible to human eyes. They include such forms of **electromagnetic radiation** as **radio waves, infrared light, ultraviolet light, X rays, and gamma rays.** Quasars also give off fast-moving jets of positively charged particles called protons and negatively charged particles called electrons.

Scientists have found that quasars are the fastest-moving objects in the universe. They and their surrounding galaxies are traveling away from us at incredible speeds. Some scientists estimate that they are moving as fast as 30,000 miles (48,000 kilometers) per second.

The quasar PKS 0637-752 appears as it did 6 billion years ago in an image taken by the Chandra X-ray Observatory. The quasar shines with the energy of 10 trillion suns, though it is smaller in area than the solar system. Astronomers think a supermassive black hole is the source of its energy.

DID YOU KNOW?

A quasar is so powerful it can outshine an entire galaxy.

Radio waves surge from Cygnus A, a type of quasar powered by a black hole, in an image from the Fermi Gamma-ray Space Telescope. Scientists classify quasars as active galaxies that give off tremendous energy in many wavelengths.

Dust particles tumble through the wind from a quasar in an artist's illustration. Some astronomers believe that quasars in the early universe created the dust particles and specks of minerals needed for the formation of stars.

HOW ARE QUASARS AND BLACK HOLES RELATED?

THE SOURCE OF POWER

Most of the gases spiraling around a **black hole** get sucked in by the black hole's **gravity.** But some of the gas is expelled at tremendous speeds. Scientists see a connection between black holes that emit high-energy particles and waves and the presence of **quasars.** Close to the center of a black hole, two extremely energetic jets of matter shoot outward, extending perhaps millions of **light-years** into space.

Scientists believe that quasars form near black holes that have somewhere between 1 million and 1 billion times the *mass* (amount of matter) of the sun. Such an incredible amount of mass is needed to provide the energy that makes quasars so bright.

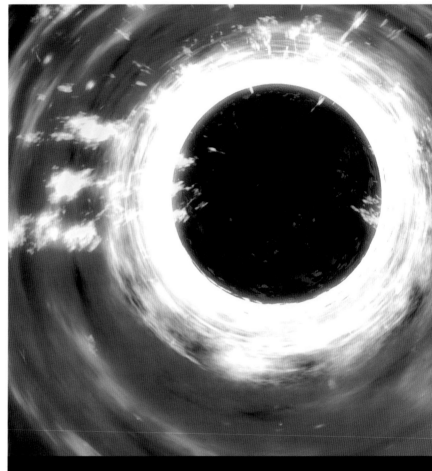

Material spiraling into the center of a black hole gives off a tremendous amount of energy, as shown in an artist's illustration.

DID YOU KNOW?

The largest black hole ever observed has the mass of 14 billion suns.

38 Explore the Universe

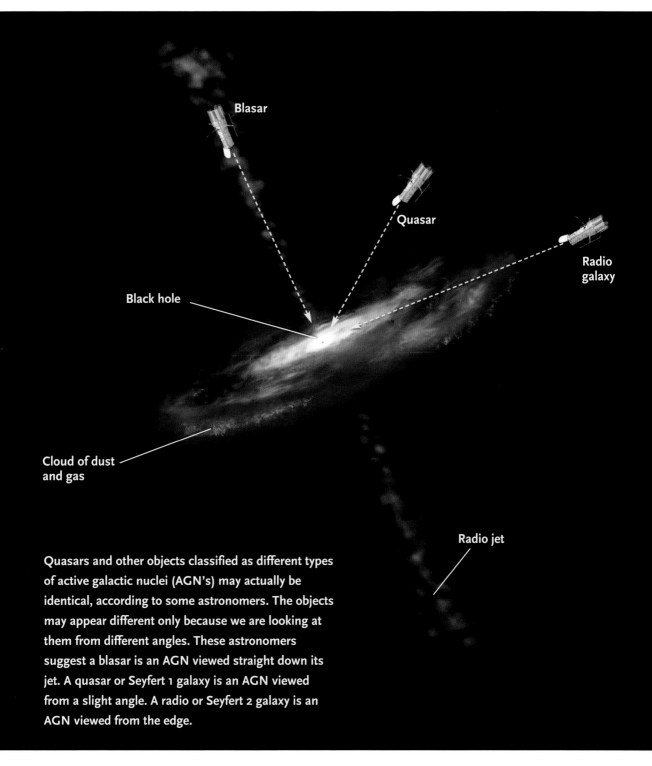

Blasar

Quasar

Radio galaxy

Black hole

Cloud of dust and gas

Radio jet

Quasars and other objects classified as different types of active galactic nuclei (AGN's) may actually be identical, according to some astronomers. The objects may appear different only because we are looking at them from different angles. These astronomers suggest a blasar is an AGN viewed straight down its jet. A quasar or Seyfert 1 galaxy is an AGN viewed from a slight angle. A radio or Seyfert 2 galaxy is an AGN viewed from the edge.

HOW FAR AWAY ARE QUASARS?

THE EARLY UNIVERSE

One way that scientists calculate the vast distances of space is by using a measurement called a **light-year.** A light-year is the distance that light travels in one year. It is equal to about 5.88 trillion miles (9.46 trillion kilometers).

Scientists think that **quasars** began to form about 13 billion years ago. This was about 700 million years after the **big bang,** the event that is believed to have started the expansion of the universe. Light from the farthest known quasar, referred to as PC1247+3406, has traveled more than 12 billion light-years to reach the Earth. This means that the **visible light** we see from this quasar today is really what the quasar looked like about 12 billion years ago. The nearest quasar identified so far, which is called 3C273, is an estimated 1.5 billion light-years from Earth.

Life could not exist on Earth if a quasar were located anywhere within our **galaxy.** Quasars are thousands of times brighter than our entire galaxy and give off tremendous amounts of energy. A quasar within even tens of light-years of Earth would destroy all life as we know it.

The most distant quasar ever observed appears as a small red dot (arrow) in an image taken by the Keck Observatory in Hawaii. The light from this object traveled more than 13 billion miles to reach Earth.

The active center of a quasar galaxy is thought to be powered by a supermassive black hole.

Quasars are so far away from Earth that their
light takes billions of years to reach us.

A jet of highly energized particles more than 100,000
light-years long shoots from the first known quasar,
which was discovered in 1963. The length of the jet
equals the width of the Milky Way Galaxy. Colors in
the jet in the composite photograph represent
various forms of light collected by various space
telescopes. Blue represents X rays observed by the
Chandra X-ray Observatory. Yellow represents
infrared light observed by the Spitzer Space
Telescope. Green represents visible light observed by
the Hubble Space Telescope.

UNITS OF
ASTRONOMICAL DISTANCE

1 astronomical unit = 150.0 million kilometers = 93.0 million miles = 0.0000158 light-years = 0.00000485 parsecs

1 light-year = 9.46 trillion kilometers = 5.88 trillion miles = 63,200 astronomical units = 0.307 parsecs

1 parsec = 30.9 trillion kilometers = 19.2 trillion miles = 206,000 astronomical units = 3.26 light-years

HOW BIG ARE QUASARS?

SMALL BUT POWERFUL

Distance makes **quasars** hard to observe. However, scientists think that most quasars cannot be much wider than the **solar system.** The solar system is about 50 **astronomical units (AU's)** across. One astronomical unit is the average distance between Earth and the sun—about 93 million miles (150 million kilometers). Quasars are incredibly compact, compared with the typical size of a **galaxy.**

Despite their size, quasars have considerable **mass** compared with other objects in the universe. Mass refers to the amount of matter in an object. Quasars may contain as much mass as several billion suns. The greater the mass of an object, the more powerful its **gravity** is. Therefore, quasars have tremendous gravitational pull for the amount of space they occupy.

A beam of high-energy particles erupting from a quasar galaxy extends about 1 million light-years into space and is thousands of times as large as the quasar itself. The quasar itself remains hidden within the bright galactic center in an image taken by the Chandra X-ray Observatory.

DID YOU KNOW?

The Chandra X-ray Observatory is a member of NASA's "Great Observatories." The other members include the Compton Gamma-ray Observatory, the Hubble Space Telescope, and the Spitzer Space Telescope.

It is difficult to know the actual size of quasars, but we do know that they probably get no bigger than the size of the solar system.

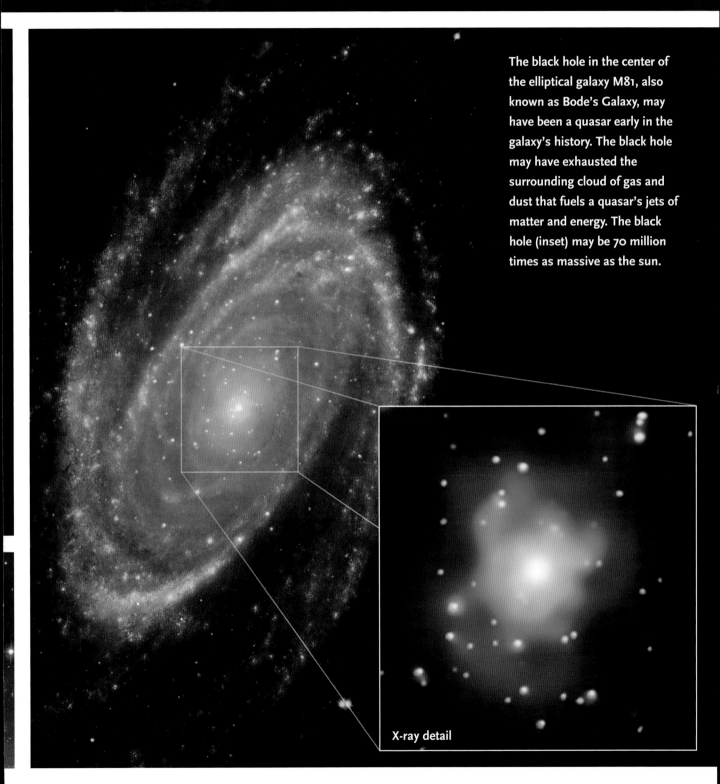

The black hole in the center of the elliptical galaxy M81, also known as Bode's Galaxy, may have been a quasar early in the galaxy's history. The black hole may have exhausted the surrounding cloud of gas and dust that fuels a quasar's jets of matter and energy. The black hole (inset) may be 70 million times as massive as the sun.

X-ray detail

THE HEART OF A GALAXY

In recent years, the Hubble Space Telescope has revealed that **quasars** often reside in a **galaxy** that has collided with another galaxy. However, scientists have also found quasars in galaxies where there are no signs of a violent interaction with another galaxy. This discovery has complicated our understanding of how quasars are created.

Many scientists think that there were more quasars long ago, when the universe was young. They estimate that quasars first appeared 13 billion years ago, about 700 million years after the **big bang,** the event that scientists believe started the expansion of the universe.

Quasars may have been more common long ago because the fuel that feeds them, dust and gas, was also more common then. As the dust and gas were used to make **stars, planets,** and other objects, the quasars lost their fuel and became less active.

The collision of galaxies, such as those in Seyfert's Sextet, may cause the galaxies' central supermassive black holes to merge into an even-larger black hole.

Scientists believe that quasars may develop when two galaxies get so close that they interact in a violent way, sometimes by colliding.

Clouds of hot, X-ray-producing gas traveling at high speeds, called a superwind, are expelled from the center of a galaxy in an artist's illustration. Such superwinds may be created when galaxies collide and push gas toward the black hole at the center of a galaxy. Over time, the superwind drives off the gas, leaving little fuel for the growth of the black hole.

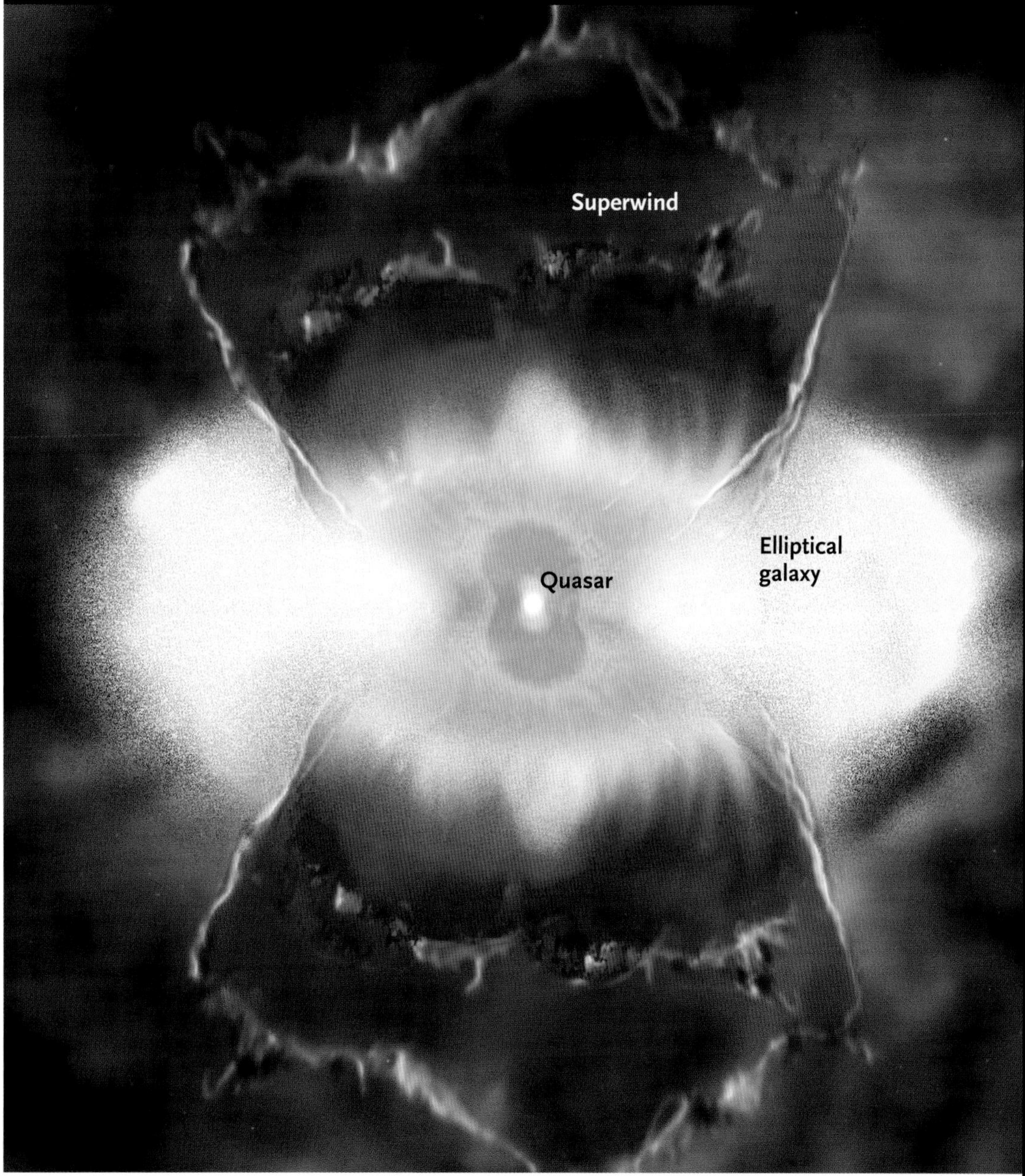

Superwind

Quasar

Elliptical galaxy

WHEN AND HOW WERE QUASARS FIRST DISCOVERED?

DISTANT RADIO WAVES

By the early 1960's, scientists had detected **radio waves** in space but could not determine the source of the waves. At first, they thought they were dealing with a strange type of **star.** In 1962, a British astronomer named Cyril Hazard discovered radio waves streaming from a specific "star" that also gave off **visible light.** This light did not resemble the light coming from other stars. A year later, in 1963, the Dutch-born American astronomer Maarten Schmidt determined that the light was coming from something much farther away and much brighter than the stars in our **galaxy.** Astronomers then realized they had found something new. The first **quasar** had been discovered. Since then, thousands of quasars have been found.

One reason quasars puzzle scientists is that their light shows extreme **redshift.** Redshift refers to the movement of light toward the red end of light's **spectrum.** When scientists look at the light from an object in space, the amount of redshift tells them how fast the object is moving and how far away it is. The light from quasars indicates that they are very distant from Earth and are moving away from us rapidly.

A radio telescope, similar to those of the Australia Telescope Compact Array near Narrabri, was the first to identify quasars as the source of mysterious radio waves from space.

Quasars were discovered in the early 1960's, after
years of observation and scientific analysis.

Many of the galaxies in an
image of the early universe
called the Hubble Deep Field
are likely quasars. Scientists
believe quasars were more
common in the distant past
than they are today.

Visible light—the light we
can see—is only one
section of the spectrum.
The light from objects far
from Earth and moving
away from us rapidly is
shifted toward the redder
end of the visible light
spectrum.

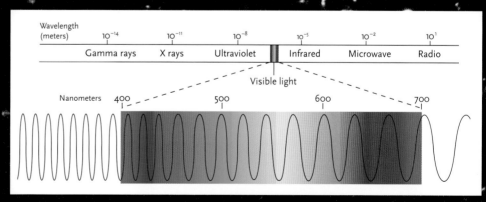

WHY DO SCIENTISTS STUDY QUASARS?

Images of quasars, such as these from the Mount Wilson Observatory in California, help astronomers gather clues about the nature of the early universe.

3C 48

3C 147

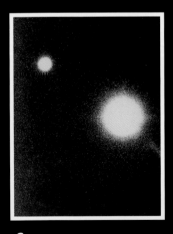

3C 273

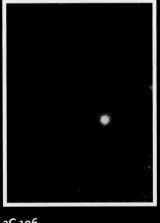

3C 196

STUDYING THE EARLY UNIVERSE

Because the light from **quasars** originated so long ago, studying quasars can help scientists observe what the universe was like early in its history. This brings us closer to an understanding of how the universe evolved.

Also, a quasar is so far away and so bright, it acts somewhat like a flashlight, illuminating everything that lies between it and Earth. This helps scientists study the dust, gas, and larger objects that fill our universe.

Scientists believe that the center of a quasar is a **black hole.** However, scientists also know there are many black holes in the universe, including many in our **galaxy.** Why are there so many black holes close to us, when quasars are all far away? This question has scientists wondering what really goes on in the center of a quasar.

DID YOU KNOW?

A team of scientists has calculated that the largest mass a black hole could contain would be equal to 50 billion suns.

The study of quasars can provide new information about the history of the universe.

The jets of energy associated with a quasar do not always erupt in a continuous stream. The jet from quasar 3C 273 is being shot out in spurts, as shown in an image from the Chandra X-ray Observatory.

WHY IS STEPHEN HAWKING IMPORTANT TO THE STUDY OF BLACK HOLES?

A BLACK HOLE SCHOLAR

Stephen Hawking is a British scientist who is generally regarded as one of the greatest minds in physics since Albert Einstein. In his quest to find out more about the origins of the universe, he has made discoveries that have changed the way scientists view space. Hawking has devoted his life to studying **black holes** and other strange features of the universe. He has also tried hard to communicate his knowledge in a simplified way so that the general public can understand these often complex and difficult ideas.

Hawking suffers from amyotrophic lateral sclerosis, an incurable disease of the nervous system. He cannot speak, nor can he move more than a few hand and face muscles. However, using a wheelchair equipped with a computer voice simulator, he has continued to work and travel.

Stephen Hawking is considered one of the greatest physicists of the last 100 years. His most renowned work is in the field of black holes.

Stephen Hawking has delved deeper into the mysteries of black holes than perhaps any other scientist.

The merging of two supermassive black holes in the galaxy NGC 6240 (colorized in orange and red) is captured in a composite image from the Chandra X-ray Observatory and the Hubble Space Telescope.

HOW LONG DOES A BLACK HOLE EXIST?

A LONG LIFE

For decades, most scientists believed that because nothing can escape the **gravitational** pull of a **black hole,** it would never come to an end. Now some scientists think that black holes lose **mass** (amount of matter) over time, until they finally evaporate.

The physicist Albert Einstein predicted that particles of matter and antimatter can appear spontaneously, when energy becomes matter. Einstein described how energy can become matter in his famous equation $E = mc^2$, where E is energy, m is mass, and c is the speed of light. The two particles annihilate each other almost instantly. British physicist Stephen Hawking suggested that if these particles appeared next to an **event horizon,** one might escape while the other fell into the black hole. The particle that fell into the event horizon would actually cause the black hole to lose mass. A black hole starved of ordinary gas and other matter would slowly lose mass through this **Hawking radiation.** Eventually, the black hole could disappear.

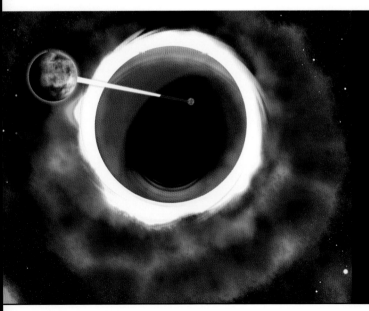

A particle of matter escapes a black hole while its complementary antiparticle falls into the event horizon in an artist's illustration. The captured antiparticle, called Hawking radiation, could eventually cause the evaporation of the black hole, according to theories by Stephen Hawking.

Until recently, scientists thought that black holes could survive forever. Now, some scientists believe black holes have a finite life span.

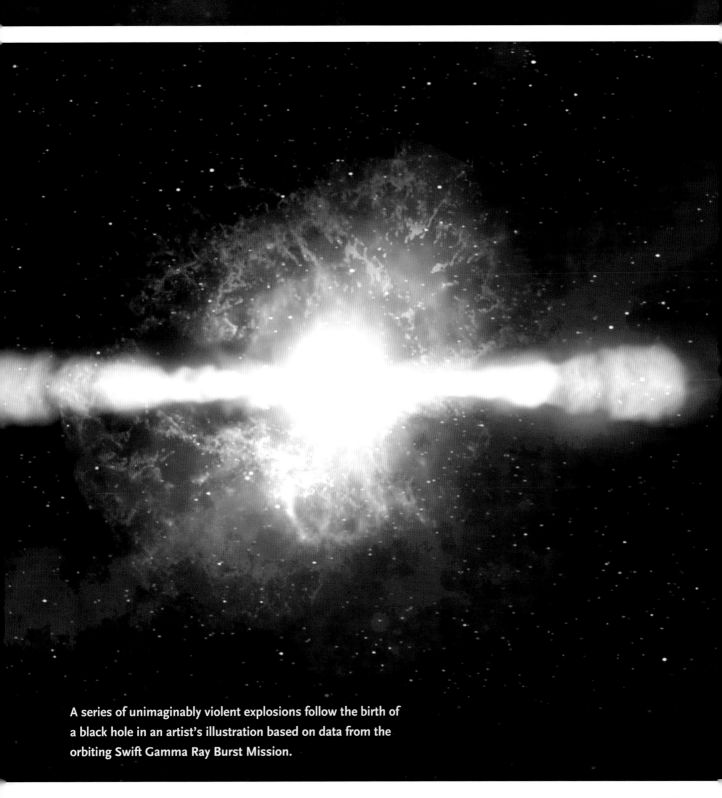

A series of unimaginably violent explosions follow the birth of a black hole in an artist's illustration based on data from the orbiting Swift Gamma Ray Burst Mission.

AN UNCOMFORTABLE SITUATION

If a person were able to survive a trip to a **black hole,** he or she would be pulled toward its center in the same way that anything else, including light, is pulled. If the person were falling toward the black hole's **event horizon** feet-first, his or her appearance would begin to look quite odd. The **gravitational** pull on the feet would be stronger than the pull on the head. As a result, the feet would become longer and move farther away from the upper parts of the body. The difference in gravitational pull would cause the entire body to stretch. The person would continue to get thinner and longer. This phenomenon is sometimes referred to as *spaghettification*.

Upon passing through the event horizon, the person's strangely shaped body would be sucked into the black hole's **singularity.** Once inside the black hole, the person's body would be stretched and pulled apart into the smallest particles of matter possible.

Even though the person would enter the singularity approaching the speed of light, time would actually slow down for that person if viewed by an outside observer, according to Albert Einstein's theories about space and time.

Speculating about entering a black hole may be fun. Unfortunately, the reality is a person would probably be pulled into tiny pieces even before he or she reached the event horizon, let alone the singularity.

A person who fell into a black hole would be broken into subatomic particles by the intense gravitational pull.

A person falling into a black hole would be pulled and stretched before falling into the singularity. This stretching is often called spaghettification.

WHY DO SCIENTISTS CONTINUE TO STUDY BLACK HOLES?

UNDERSTANDING THE UNIVERSE

Scientists know much more than they used to about **black holes** in particular and the universe in general. However, there is probably an immense amount of information still to be gathered and understood.

For example, scientists believe that supermassive black holes govern **star** formation in **galaxies** through heating gas. Also, they play some role in the formation of galaxies. In addition, black holes offer evidence in support of Einstein's theory of relativity.

Black holes are extreme objects that create some of the most energetic events in the universe. And the ordinary laws of physics may break down inside the event horizon. Studying such extremes may help us to understand the basic laws that govern our universe.

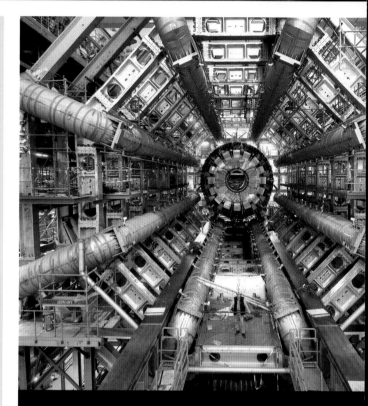

Some scientists have speculated that particle accelerators like the Large Hadron Collider could create tiny black holes. Even if this occurred, scientists generally agree that such black holes would vanish almost instantly and pose no threat to the machine or to people.

DID YOU KNOW?

The Large Hadron Collider is the single largest machine in the world.

Computer simulations of black holes help scientists understand the behavior of these unusual objects.

WHAT IS A MICRO BLACK HOLE?

A TINY HOLE IN SPACE

Micro black holes, also called mini black holes, are thought to contain as much *mass* (amount of matter) as a large mountain. This amount of mass is relatively low compared with the mass of a typical **star.** But even with the mass of a mountain, the black hole would be microscopic.

The existence of micro black holes has been one of the many theories put forth by Stephen Hawking. Hawking believes that these tiny structures were created almost immediately after the **big bang,** the event that is thought to have caused the expansion of the universe. The temperature of the universe was unbelievably high at that moment. Hawking theorizes that under such extreme temperatures, small amounts of matter might have been compressed to points of extreme density, leading to the birth of micro black holes. These low-mass micro black holes would have evaporated already because of **Hawking radiation,** but astronomers hope they might detect the burst of energy given off by the evaporation of larger micro black holes.

Some scientists think that micro black holes could be particularly common in certain parts of the universe, such as the outer reaches of our **galaxy.**

COSMIC EPOCHS

Scientists believe the universe was created in a massive explosion called the big bang 13.7 billion years ago. Some scientists, including Stephen Hawking, believe micro black holes may have been created in the initial few milliseconds after the big bang but evaporated quickly.

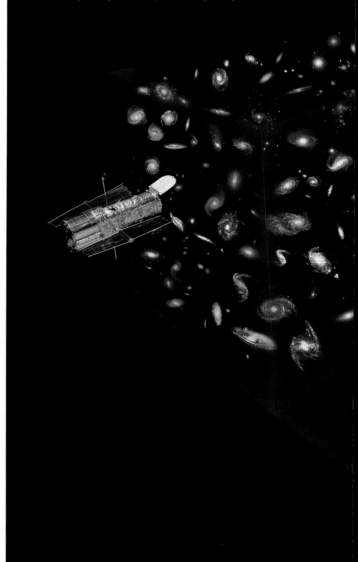

Scientists believe that galaxies might contain micro
black holes, tiny versions of their larger cousins.
A micro black hole is probably the size of an atom.

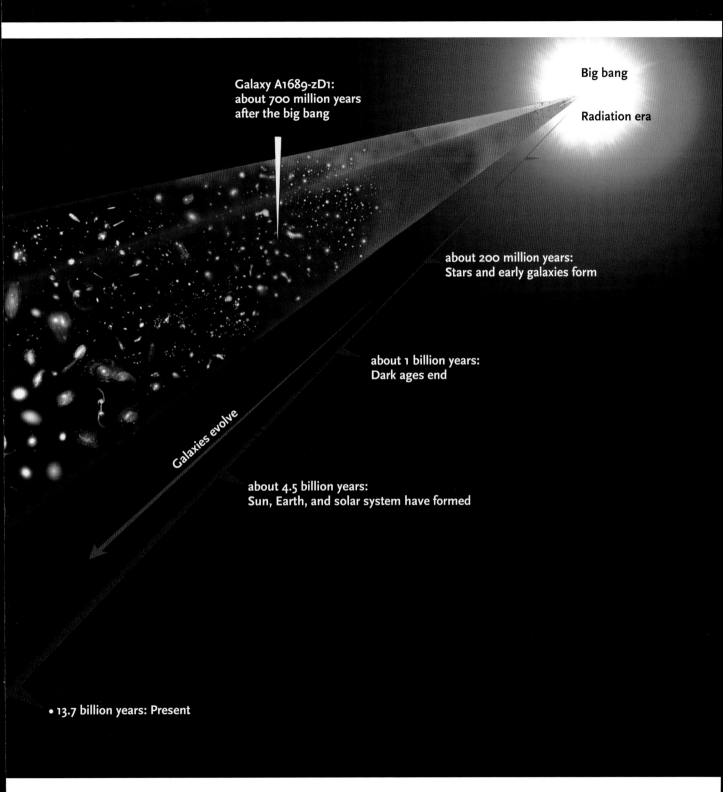

Big bang

Galaxy A1689-zD1:
about 700 million years
after the big bang

Radiation era

about 200 million years:
Stars and early galaxies form

about 1 billion years:
Dark ages end

Galaxies evolve

about 4.5 billion years:
Sun, Earth, and solar system have formed

• 13.7 billion years: Present

GLOSSARY

Accretion disk – A disk-shaped formation of gases or other interstellar matter around a massive body such as a star.

Active galactic nucleus (AGN) – The extremely bright core of an active galaxy. AGN's radiate more energy than does the rest of the stars, gas, and dust in the galaxy. AGN's are probably powered by supermassive black holes.

Active galaxy – A galaxy that gives off vast amounts of radiation from its core.

Astronomical unit (AU) – The average distance between Earth and the sun, or about 93 million miles (150 million kilometers).

Big bang – The cosmic explosion that scientists believe began the expansion of the universe.

Binary stars – Stars that orbit each other.

Black hole – The collapsed core of a massive star. The gravity of a black hole is so strong that not even light can escape.

Core – The dense, hot center of a star.

Electromagnetic radiation – Any form of light, ranging from radio waves, to microwaves, to infrared light, to visible light, to ultraviolet light, to X rays, to gamma rays. Radio waves have the longest wavelength and lowest energy; gamma rays have the shortest wavelength and highest energy.

Event horizon – The boundary of a black hole where the pull of gravity becomes stronger than any other force.

Galaxy – A vast system of stars, gas, dust, and other matter held together in space by mutual gravitational attraction.

Gamma rays – The form of light with the shortest wavelengths. Gamma rays are invisible to the unaided eye.

Gravity – The force of attraction that acts between all objects because of their mass.

Hawking radiation – Radiation given off by black holes, as described in the theories of physicist Stephen Hawking. A black hole may give off Hawking radiation when virtual particles form near the event horizon. If one particle is captured, it results in a loss of mass to the black hole. A black hole may eventually evaporate due to Hawking radiation.

Infrared light – A form of light with long wavelengths. Also called heat radiation. Infrared is invisible to the unaided eye.

Light-year – The distance light travels in a vacuum in one year. One light-year is equal to 5.88 trillion miles (9.46 trillion kilometers).

Mass – The amount of matter in an object.

Micro black hole – A black hole with far less mass than a conventional black hole. Micro black holes were described in the theories of Stephen Hawking. They are believed to have formed immediately following the big bang. Conventional black holes form when massive stars collapse after exhausting their fuel.

Neutron star – A star that has collapsed into a small area with extremely high mass. Neutron stars form from the remains of massive stars that have exploded in supernovae.

Observatory – A structure used to observe the heavens.

Optical – Of or relating to visible light.

Quasar – An extremely bright object at the center of some distant galaxies. The word *quasar* is a shortened form of *quasi-stellar radio source*. Quasars give off enormous amounts of energy in the form of visible light, ultraviolet light, infrared rays, X rays, gamma rays, and in some cases, radio waves. Astronomers believe quasars are powered by supermassive black holes.

Radio waves – The form of light with the longest wavelengths. Radio waves are invisible to the unaided eye.

Schwarzschild radius – The size at which the gravitational forces of a collapsing body in space become so strong that they prevent the escape of any matter or radiation. An object that collapses to a size smaller than its Schwarzschild radius becomes a black hole. The Schwarzschild radius of a black hole singularity is called the event horizon.

Singularity – The point at the center of a black hole where the core has collapsed to a space smaller than an atom.

Solar mass – A unit of measure used to describe the mass of bodies in space. One solar mass is equal to the mass of the sun.

Space-time – Space conceived as a continuum of four dimensions, namely length, width, height, and time. Physicist Albert Einstein's theories of relativity showed that space and time are fundamentally joined.

Spectrum, spectra – Light divided into its different wavelengths. A spectrum may provide astronomers with information about a heavenly body's chemical composition, motion, and distance.

Star – A huge, shining ball in space that produces a tremendous amount of visible light and other forms of energy.

Ultraviolet light – A form of light with short wavelengths. Ultraviolet light is invisible to the unaided eye.

Visible light – The form of light human beings can see with their eyes.

Wavelength – The distance between successive crests, or peaks, of a wave. Wavelength is used to distinguish among different forms of light. Radio waves have the longest wavelengths, and gamma rays have the shortest wavelengths.

White dwarf – A star that has exhausted its fuel. A typical white dwarf has about 60 percent as much mass as the sun but is no larger than the Earth.

X rays – A form of light with short wavelengths. X rays are invisible to the unaided eye.

FOR MORE INFORMATION

WEB SITES
Black Holes

http://hubblesite.org/explore_astronomy/black_holes

NASA's HubbleSite on black holes features videos of how they are formed and how they can be found, plus an encyclopedia that answers common questions about them.

Black Holes and Quasars

http://curious.astro.cornell.edu/blackholes.php

An astronomer from Cornell University explains and answers people's questions about black holes and quasars.

How Black Holes Work

http://www.howstuffworks.com/black-hole.htm

HowStuffWorks gives a basic introduction to black holes, with pictures of several types.

The Mysteries of Deep Space

http://www.spacetoday.org/DeepSpace.html

Choose from such topics as quasars, nebulae, magnetars, and black holes to read the latest articles on research in the field.

BOOKS
Beyond the Solar System: From Red Giants to Black Holes by Steve Parker (Rosen Central, 2008)

Black Holes by Ker Than (Children's Press, 2009)

Death Stars, Weird Galaxies, and a Quasar-Spangled Universe by Karen Taschek (University of New Mexico Press, 2006)

Mysterious Universe: Supernovae, Dark Energy, and Black Holes by Ellen B. Jackson (Houghton Mifflin Books, 2008)

The Mystery of Black Holes by Chris Oxlade (Heinemann Library, 2005)

INDEX

ACKNOWLEDGMENTS

The publishers acknowledge the following sources for illustrations. Credits read from top to bottom, left to right, on their respective pages. All illustrations, maps, charts, and diagrams were prepared by the staff unless otherwise noted.

Cover: NASA/CXC/CfA/R.Kraft et al. (x-ray), MPIfR/ESO/APEX/A. Weiss et al. (submillimeter), ESO/WFI (optical)

1 NASA/Dana Berry, SkyWorks Digital

4-5 X-ray: NASA/CXC/GSFC/M. Corcoran et al.; Optical: NASA/STScI

6-7 NASA/CXC/CfA/R. Kraft; AP Images; NASA/Dana Berry, SkyWorks Digital

8-9 NASA/CXC/M. Weiss; NASA/CXC/M. Weiss; NASA/CXC/M. Weiss; NASA and Jon Morse (Univ. of Colorado)

10-11 © Print Collection/Alamy Images; CXC; Russell et al. 2007, MNRAS, 376, 1341 (http://adsabs.harvard.edu/abs/2007MNRAS.376.1341R) and Stirling et al. 2001, MNRAS, 327, 1273 (http://adsabs.harvard.edu/abs/2001MNRAS.327.1273S)

12-13 NASA/CXC/SAO/M. Karovska et al.; NRAO/AUI/NSF/J. Condon et al.; Digital Sky Survey/U.K. Schmidt Image/STScI; NRAO/AUI/NSF/J. Van Gorkom/Schminovich et al.; X-ray: NASA/CXC/SAO/M. Karovska et al.; Optical: Digital Sky Survey/U.K. Schmidt Image/STScI

14-15 WORLD BOOK illustration by Matt Carrington; WORLD BOOK illustration by Matt Carrington; © 2006 James Overduin, Pancho Eckels & Bob Kahn, Gravity Probe B Image Archives, Stanford Univ.

16-17 NASA/Goddard Space Flight Center; Marble Collectors Unlimited; NASA and K. Gebhardt (Lick Observatory)

18-19 © Mehau Kulyk, Photo Researchers; © Alan Goulet, istockphoto

20-21 Ann Feild, Space Telescope Science Institute; NASA/WORLD BOOK illustration

22-23 Tim Jones/UT-Austin after K. Cordes & S. Brown (STScI); Falcke/Fußhöller, Radboud Univ. Nijmegen/MPIfR Bonn 2004 (http://www.astro.ru.nl/~falcke/bh/sld12.html)

24-25 NASA/CXC/M. Weiss; X-ray (NASA/CXC/Columbia/F. Bauer et al.); Visible light (NASA/STScI/UMD/A. Wilson et al.)

26-27 NASA/CXC/MIT/F. K. Baganoff et al.; NASA/CXC/CfA/R. Hickox et al.; NASA/JPL-Caltech/E. Daddi (CEA, Saclay)

28-29 NASA/JPL/California Institute of Technology; NASA/CXC/M. Weiss; NASA/CXC/M. Weiss

30-31 NASA/CXC/M. Weiss; NOAO/AURA/NSF and P. Marenfeld; NASA/CXC/AlfA/D. Hudson & T. Reiprich et al.

32-33 NASA/SOHO; NASA/J. Harrington et al.; NASA/CXC/M. Weiss

34-35 WORLD BOOK illustration by Ernest Norcia; WORLD BOOK illustration by Matt Carrington; NASA, ESA, Richard Ellis (Caltech) and Jean-Paul Kneib (Observatoire Midi-Pyrenees)

36-37 NASA/CXC/SAO; NRAO; NASA/JPL-Caltech/T. Pyle (SSC)

38-39 NASA; NASA/Aurore Simmonet, Sonoma State Univ.

40-41 Stephen Kent, SDSS Collaboration; NASA/JPL-Caltech/T. Pyle (SSC); NASA/JPL-Caltech/Yale Univ.

42-43 NASA/CXC/A. Siemiginowska (CfA)/J. Bechtold (Univ. Ariz.); X-ray: NASA/CXC/Wisconsin/D. Pooley & CfA/A. Zezas; Optical: NASA/ESA/CfA/A. Zezas; UV: NASA/JPL-Caltech/CfA/J. Huchra et al.; IR: NASA/JPL-Caltech/CfA

44-45 NASA, J. English (Univ. Manitoba), S. Hunsberger, S. Zonak, J. Charlton, S. Gallagher (PSU), and L. Frattare (STScI); NASA/CXC/M. Weiss

46-47 © Joe Gough, Dreamstime; NASA and Robert Williams and the Hubble Deep Field Team (STScI); WORLD BOOK illustration

48-49 Palomar Observatory/California Institute of Technology; NASA/CXC/SAO/H. Marshall et al.

50-51 © Menahem Kahana, AFP/Getty Images; X-ray (NASA/CXC/MIT/C. Canizares, M. Nowak); Optical (NASA/STScI)

52-53 WORLD BOOK illustration by Matt Carrington; NASA/GSFC/Dana Berry

54-55 NASA; WORLD BOOK illustration/NASA

56-57 © Maximilien Brice, CERN; KIPAC/SLAC/M. Alvarez, T. Abel and J. Wise

58-59 NASA, ESA, and A. Feild (STScI)